2/18 BC

D1592354

TRAINING TO FIGHT WITH
THE PARACHUTE REGIMENT

ELITE FORCES SURVIVAL GUIDE SERIES

Elite Survival
Survive in the Desert with the French Foreign Legion
Survive in the Arctic with the Royal Marine Commandos
Survive in the Mountains with the U.S. Rangers and Army
  Mountain Division
Survive in the Jungle with the Special Forces "Green Berets"
Survive in the Wilderness with the Canadian and Australian
  Special Forces
Survive at Sea with the U.S. Navy SEALs
Training to Fight with the Parachute Regiment
The World's Best Soldiers

Elite Operations and Training
Escape and Evasion
Surviving Captivity with the U.S. Air Force
Hostage Rescue with the SAS
How to Pass Elite Forces Selection
Learning Mental Endurance with the U.S. Marines

Special Forces Survival Guidebooks
Survival Equipment
Navigation and Signaling
Surviving Natural Disasters
Using Ropes and Knots
Survival First Aid
Trapping, Fishing, and Plant Food
Urban Survival Techniques

TRAINING TO FIGHT WITH
THE PARACHUTE REGIMENT

CHRIS McNAB

Introduction by Colonel John T. Carney. Jr., USAF–Ret.
President, Special Operations Warrior Foundation

MASON CREST PUBLISHERS

This edition first published in 2003
by Mason Crest Publishers Inc.
370 Reed Road, Broomall, PA, 19008

Library of Congress Cataloging-in-Publication Data available

ISBN 1-59084-007-0

Editorial and design by
Amber Books Ltd.
Bradley's Close
74–77 White Lion Street
London N1 9PF

Project Editor Chris Stone
Designer Simon Thompson
Picture Research Lisa Wren

Printed and bound in Malaysia

10 9 8 7 6 5 4 3 2 1

ACKNOWLEDGMENT

For authenticating this book, the Publishers would like to thank the Public Affairs Offices of the U.S. Special Operations Command, MacDill AFB, FL.; Army Special Operations Command, Fort Bragg, N.C.; Navy Special Warfare Command, Coronado, CA.; and the Air Force Special Operations Command, Hurlbert Field, FL.

IMPORTANT NOTICE
The survival techniques and information described in this publication are for use in dire circumstances where the safety of the individual is at risk. Accordingly, the publisher cannot accept any responsibility for any prosecution or proceedings brought or instituted against any person or body as a result of the uses or misuses of the techniques and information within.

DEDICATION
This book is dedicated to those who perished in the terrorist attacks of September 11, 2001, and to the Special Forces soldiers who continually serve to defend freedom.

Picture Credits
Military Picture Library: 8; **TRH**: 6, 11, 12, 19, 22, 27, 28, 30, 31, 32, 35, 36, 38, 39, 42, 44, 46, 48, 50, 52, 54, 56, 57, 58, 59, 60, 64, 66, 67, 68, 69, 72, 75, 77, 78, 80, 84, 86, 87; /P. MacDonald: 41; /US Navy: 16; /H.M. Roberts: 34; /A. Rogers: 33; **US Dept. of Defense**: 20, 74
Illustrations courtesy of Amber Books.
Front cover: TRH (both)

CONTENTS

11 JUL 2005

INTRODUCTION

Elite forces are the tip of Freedom's spear. These small, special units are universally the first to engage, whether on reconnaissance missions into denied territory for larger, conventional forces or in direct action, surgical operations, preemptive strikes, retaliatory action, and hostage rescues. They lead the way in today's war on terrorism, the war on drugs, the war on transnational unrest, and in humanitarian operations as well as nation building. When large scale warfare erupts, they offer theater commanders a wide variety of unique, unconventional options.

Most such units are regionally oriented, acclimated to the culture and conversant in the languages of the areas where they operate. Since they deploy to those areas regularly, often for combined training exercises with indigenous forces, these elite units also serve as peacetime "global scouts" and "diplomacy multipliers," a beacon of hope for the democratic aspirations of oppressed peoples all over the globe.

Elite forces are truly "quiet professionals": their actions speak louder than words. They are self-motivated, self-confident, versatile, seasoned, mature individuals who rely on teamwork more than daring-do. Unfortunately, theirs is dangerous work. Since "Desert One"—the 1980 attempt to rescue hostages from the U.S. embassy in Tehran, for instance—American special operations forces have suffered casualties in real world operations at close to fifteen times the rate of U.S. conventional forces. By the very nature of the challenges which face special operations forces, training for these elite units has proven even more hazardous.

Thus it's with special pride that I join you in saluting the brave men and women who volunteer to serve in and support these magnificent units and who face such difficult challenges ahead.

Colonel John T. Carney, Jr., USAF–Ret.
President, Special Operations Warrior Foundation

Exhausted recruits try to catch their breath after one of the Regiment's 10-mile (16-km) speed marches.

THE BRITISH PARAS

The red beret worn by the British Parachute Regiment is a world-renowned symbol of an elite military unit. From the epic battle at Arnhem in World War II to the actions at Goose Green and Wireless Ridge during the Falklands conflict, the Paras have proved they are second to none.

Just after lunch on Sunday, September 17, 1944, the sound of an apparently vast armada of aircraft brought the people of the Dutch town of Arnhem into the streets. At this time, the Dutch were waiting for liberation from the Germans as the Allies fought their way across occupied Europe. To the west of the town, it appeared to be snowing as thousands of British paratroopers left their aircraft in the largest parachute operation ever to be mounted. The people of Arnhem had not expected to see the Allies so quickly. The front was still 80 miles (130 km) away and the Germans were digging in for a hard fight.

The British Paras went to Arnhem to capture a vital bridge before the Germans could destroy it. They were then meant to hold the bridge until the main force of Allies could reach them. Yet what the Paras did not know as they parachuted deep behind enemy lines, was that huge numbers of elite German troops, many armed with tanks, were resting in the area.

All Paras are experts in communication and navigation. These Paras are using a high-frequency radio during a combat exercise.

The problems began early on. The Paras were landed by both parachute and 319 special gliders, which flew silently into the drop zone. In the initial landings, 39 gliders were missing. Yet their biggest problem appeared to be the thousands of civilians lining the streets, thinking that they were being liberated.

The Germans reacted quickly. By **1500 hours**, the Ninth SS Panzer Division was moving toward the Allied landing grounds and setting up a defensive ring around the town of Arnhem.

By late afternoon, most of the British paratroops were engaged in bitter street fighting. As the light faded, two smaller bridges had been blown up in their faces. Even worse, the Germans had split the Para force into two halves.

The main bridge itself became the scene of great courage for the Paras.

A 1956 Para with combat kit (80 lb/36.3 kg) including backpack, sleeping bag, and 9-mm Sten Mk V submachine gun.

They had captured the northern end. Twice they tried to take the southern end but were driven back by heavy machine-gun fire. The battle started a fire in a German ammunition dump. This spread to four trucks and finally the bridge itself. With the night eerily illuminated by the burning bridge, further attacks were impossible. The Paras withdrew to set up positions in buildings overlooking the northern end.

Nine days of unmatched courage followed as the Paras desperately resisted the German attacks and awaited the arrival of the Allied main force. More Paras were dropped into the battle. But when the **RAF** appeared overhead to drop supplies, most fell

The bridge at Arnhem in September 1944, scene of one of the Parachute Regiment's most desperate, and heroic, battles of World War II. The Regiment lost hundreds of men.

Those who pass the parachute training course, known as "Basic Para," earn their "wings," a badge that goes on their uniform. The "wings" above are awarded to men from the SAS Special Forces.

into the arms of the Germans. When the ammunition ran low, German counterattacks were driven off with bayonets and sheer courage. Many of the Paras—those who were still alive anyway— were wounded but fought on.

Five **Victoria Crosses** (VCs) were won at Arnhem by the Paras. Yet these were just the greatest examples of bravery and endurance. On Monday, September 25, the survivors, without food and with only rainwater to drink, had to withdraw. Arnhem had been a military disaster, but the world now knew that the British Paras were some of the bravest fighting men ever seen.

The Paras fought in many other conflicts during World War II and many afterward. In each battle, they confirmed their reputation for military excellence. In 1982, that reputation was to be tested again. The British Falkland Islands had been seized on April 2 by Argentine forces. The British government reacted quickly. They sent a huge military force to recapture the islands, including three Royal Marine Commandos and two Parachute Regiment battalions. When the commandos and Paras splashed ashore at San Carlos on May 21, they were outnumbered by two to one and they would have to fight in a freezing climate.

The majority of the enemy were dug into trenches on two lines of mountain ridges around the island's capital, Stanley. The nearest Argentine force was 20 miles (32 km) away from where the Paras had landed at places called Darwin and Goose Green. The settlements were held by more than 1,200 men of the Argentine army. They were heavily armed and had support from attack aircraft.

In the early morning hours of May 28, the Paras began their attack after having marched more than 25 miles (40 km). At first, the resistance was light. Yet as dawn approached, enemy artillery and mortar fire increased and the Paras were showered with machine-gun bullets. The Paras had to crawl forward under the fire—at times, the Paras crawled to within 200 feet (50 m) of the Argentine positions. Then the trenches were stormed with sheer aggression and the "raw" fighting techniques of close quarter combat.

By midmorning, the battalion attack had become bogged down as a result of heavy enemy fire. The commanding officer, Lieutenant Colonel "H" Jones, moved forward to take personal command and break the deadlock. While charging forward, Jones was hit by gunfire. Still charging forward firing his submachine gun, he fell, mortally wounded. He was **posthumously** awarded the Victoria Cross.

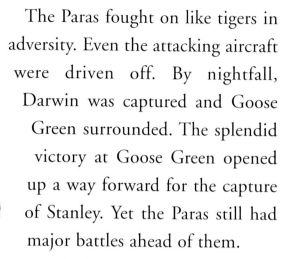

The Paras fought on like tigers in adversity. Even the attacking aircraft were driven off. By nightfall, Darwin was captured and Goose Green surrounded. The splendid victory at Goose Green opened up a way forward for the capture of Stanley. Yet the Paras still had major battles ahead of them.

The Paras took part in the final battles of the war. Late on the night of June 13, the Paras were told to capture Wireless Ridge. This was a ridge on Mount Longdon and it was very heavily defended. The Paras soon found themselves in a bloody fight with hundreds of Argentine soldiers. Fighting bunker to bunker, the Paras cleared the ridge and dug in to await enemy artillery strikes. At dawn, the Argentinians launched the only counterattack of the war. This last serious attempt to hold

A Para in the Falklands War in 1982 takes a break from the fighting. He wears Arctic combats and carries a 9-mm Sterling submachine gun.

onto the Falkland Islands was defeated, despite the fact that the Paras were seriously short of ammunition. The enemy went into full retreat. In the early afternoon, the Paras marched toward Stanley, their steel helmets replaced by the famous **red beret.**

Because of actions at places like Arnhem and the Falkland Islands, the Paras have become one of the world's most respected military units. Today, the Paras train hard to keep that reputation, and so the training regime is tough and unforgiving. In the following chapters, we will look at what a person has to do before he or she can be accepted into this elite unit.

BRAVERY AT ARNHEM

Just one example of the incredible bravery shown at Arnhem in September, 1944, can be found in a Para called Captain Queripel. He already had facial wounds when he rescued a badly injured comrade under heavy tank and artillery fire. Then he returned to lead an assault on a German position and destroyed two machine guns and a captured British antitank gun. Fighting from a ditch, Queripel's men repelled wave after wave of German soldiers. Finally, with most of his men dead or wounded, the captain, now badly wounded in both arms, remained behind to cover the withdrawal. He was last seen throwing grenades back at the Germans. His actions won him a posthumous Victoria Cross (VC).

BEING A BRITISH PARA

What makes a paratrooper different? What gives British Paras the strength and fighting power that have taken them to victory all over the world—from the freezing rain of the Falklands to the baking rocks of Saudi Arabia?

There is no doubt that a soldier needs to have something a little bit different to be a Para. He or she has to show aggression and be able to take control of a battlefield when others panic. The most obvious difference between the Parachute Regiment and other British infantry regiments is the paratrooper's parachuting role. But this is not the most important difference. To the Regiment, a parachute is just a way of getting into battle—though a very daring one. What matters is what airborne soldiers do once they hit the ground. That depends on their character and their training —it is the quality of the individual paratrooper that separates the Parachute Regiment from the rest.

This high quality is needed throughout the Regiment because **airborne operations** are so difficult and tough. The Paras have a regimental spirit and attitude that have kept them in the world's elite since its creation. Parachute missions are very expensive and complex. That is why the Paras are usually used only for the most important and dangerous missions. So every member of the

Paras are proud of the Regiment's list of battle honors, which include operations in Cyprus, Borneo, Northern Ireland, and the Falklands.

Regiment must realize that the only thing that matters is the success of every operation.

Because of this, the Parachute Regiment attaches great importance to determination—all Paras must show that they are determined to see a mission through even though the danger may be overwhelming.

Winning parachute battles usually requires a lot of courage. Even to leap out of an aircraft into empty space requires all paratroopers to find the aggression within themselves to overcome their natural fear. Once on the ground, the element of surprise is vital for the lightly equipped airborne soldier, who will probably have to fight large numbers of enemy soldiers. Often, a paratrooper may come under fire from the moment he lands on the **DZ** (Drop Zone). In order to achieve surprise, and to capture the objective before enemy reinforcements can arrive, all members of the Regiment throw themselves into battle without holding back.

This is how one Para describes it: "Our troops are more aggressive than any other troops anyway, and it all boils down to the training and the type of person needed to pass that training. We find that the aggression among our recruits is very high; they are very aggressive."

Just as aggression is vital, so too is fitness. Military parachuting is, after all, extremely hard work. According to medical experts, every parachute jump takes the same effort as eight hours' work because of the mental and physical stress. The preparation before a jump is long. All paratroopers are

Behind enemy lines, ammunition can run out. Recruits must therefore be trained in unarmed combat. Fitness regimes also promote suppleness, which is essential when making heavy landings.

Paras open their parachutes at many different heights, from as high as 27,000 feet (8,500 m) to as low as 800 feet (240 m).

briefed—told precisely what they need to know for the drop, and what they need to know in order to achieve their mission once they are on the ground. They must select and fit their own parachutes. They must practice the **drills** they need to rendezvous with the other members of their **company** after landing. They may get very little sleep before the jump. Once in the aircraft, they may doze, but up to 20 minutes before leaping through the door, they have to stand up, fully alert, with all their equipment on.

With a main parachute, a reserve parachute, and all the weapons, ammunition, and food they need for the forthcoming operation, this can amount to as much as 176 pounds (80 kg). In

Paras must be able to live off the land by hunting, finding sources of water, and constructing "hides" to remain unseen by enemy soldiers.

As soon as the Paras hit the ground, they must secure the area. This soldier from 2 Para has immediately set up his machine gun. If there is no threat, he will then pack away his parachute.

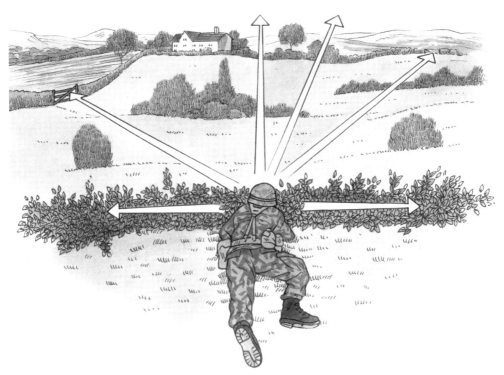

Effective reconnaissance of enemy positions is essential before the Paras can launch an attack or call in an air strike.

a bucking aircraft flying just above the treetops, this is a strenuous task—made even worse if the recruits are feeling airsick. The tension and stress involved in parachuting, and the aggression needed to actually throw themselves through the aircraft door, sap their energy even further. Then they must do the jump itself, and land without injuring themselves. However, a successful parachute jump is only the beginning.

Once they hit the ground, the Paras' job has only just begun. They must use the effect of surprise and move quickly to attack their target before the enemy can react to the parachute assault. The target is often several miles from the DZ, and the Paras are

THE U.S. PARA

Where Britain has an Airborne Brigade, the U.S. Airborne Forces has a much larger formation. The U.S. XVIII Airborne Corps has many divisions. (Brigades are only part of a division.) The spearhead of the Airborne Corps is the 82nd Airborne Division. This unit comes from the U.S. parachute troops who fought in World War II, and it wears the famous red berets of Paras around the world. The unit consists of about 16,000 men, which is three times the size of the British Parachute Regiment. It can be flown anywhere around the world by over 800 huge transport aircraft. These aircraft can even drop small tanks into battle for the airborne soldiers. The 82nd Airborne Division is based at Fort Bragg in North Carolina and is an elite unit in the U.S. armed forces.

heavily loaded with all their weapons and equipment. There are never enough aircraft to drop many vehicles. So they must walk, and walk fast, or "tab" as it is known in the Regiment. When they get to their objective, they have to attack it and take it from the enemy. They may then have to defend it for days, beating off what may be incessant enemy counterattacks.

It is no accident that the Latin motto of the Parachute Regiment is **Utrinque Paratus**—"Ready for Anything." The Regiment must at all times be able to fight in whatever situation

A Para on the troubled streets of Northern Ireland. Although the region is currently part of the United Kingdom, some parts of the Catholic community in Northern Ireland want to sever this link. This conflict of opinion has lasted for several hundred years, and military force has often been required to quell the unrest between Catholics and Protestants. The country is just a tenth of the size of New York State.

it finds itself. To do this calls for intelligence and bravery from every individual, not just from the officers and **NCOs**, but from the **Toms** as well. (A "Tom" is a private soldier in the Parachute Regiment.) In a drop, the Paras may be scattered over a wide area. Private soldiers may well be separated from their commanders and find themselves in the middle of enemy territory. In the **D-Day** drop in the early hours of June 6, 1944, for example, over 1,000 men of the 6th Airborne Division were scattered far and wide, miles from their battalions. Even so, as they struggled through marshes and bogs to get back to their units, they managed to cause destruction and confusion to German forces along the way, creating the impression of a much larger airborne landing.

In an airborne operation, there is no turning back. Once paratroopers leap through the door, they cannot simply turn around, get back on the aircraft, and go home. Miles behind enemy lines, heavily outnumbered and with the element of surprise so important, an airborne force has to succeed the first time. If it fails to achieve its mission, the force cannot go back and try again the following day. These are the reasons why the Parachute Regiment demands a high standard of its soldiers. To get the right kind of person with all these qualities is a difficult task, because an interview or medical inspection will not uncover these qualities. Ever since its creation in World War II, the Parachute Regiment has tested the fitness and strength of character of everyone who wants to be a Para. It does this in a grueling selection procedure that pushes all who go through it to their limits—the legendary **"P" Company**.

Long runs carrying heavy backpacks are a part of the grueling
selection test the Paras call "P" Company.

THE RECRUITS ARRIVE

A 10-mile (16-km) run in one hour and 45 minutes carrying over 50 pounds (23 kg). A seven-mile race over mountains helping to carry a 165-pound (75-kg) stretcher. These are just two of the events of "P" Company, tests that push a potential Para to the limits of pain and endurance.

"P" Company is hard. Any test designed to make Paras has to be. Few people in civilian life today have ever had to run with a large weight on their backs and heavy boots on their feet. So, new recruits to the Regiment spend 12 weeks building themselves up. They do this to prepare for "P" Company itself, the grueling week of tests that will decide if the recruits have what it takes to become Paras.

Most of these 12 weeks are spent at a place called the **Depot**. This is situated in Browning Barracks, Aldershot, England. The first week of recruit training takes place when the civilian and the Regiment get to know one another. It is at Aldershot railroad station that the fresh-faced civilian first meets the Regiment. It is not hard to spot new recruits for the Army as soon as they get off the train. They may not have the short hair yet and they may be trying to act confidently, but their nervous looks give them away.

Back at the Depot, the first step is to try to get all these different people into a team that works together. This begins by making all the

During the selection process, recruits must be able to complete three laps of an 18-obstacle 400-yard (366-m) course at top speed.

Up to 60 recruits sign up for each Parachute Regiment course. Less than half will make it to the passing out parade on the final day.

recruits look the same, or at least as similar as possible. A two-minute trip to the barber removes practically all their hair, and all men wear a short crew cut. In addition to getting their hair cut, the recruits spend the first two days of their training having medicals, filling in forms, and collecting **kit**. Already, they are beginning to discover how important it is to look after clothing and equipment. For the recruits, getting their uniforms is usually an exciting time, suddenly turning them from civilians into soldiers. In the Regiment's eyes, of course, it will take a little longer. Simply wearing a uniform does not make the recruits into paratroopers, and, instead of the red beret of the airborne soldier, they have to wear standard camouflaged combat caps. They will have to earn the red beret.

Not all of the new recruits decide they want to, though. Lots of recruits leave in the first few weeks because they find army life too tough. Some of the recruits have never left home before. As one of the Depot staff puts it: "For many of them, their mothers make their beds, and food has always been on the table. They have never even picked up an iron."

Many of the recruits, even those who have come straight from such pampering, will not necessarily want to leave. They rise to the challenges of the new way of life. Others, however, do not like to do the boring jobs that come with being a soldier. The excitement of wearing uniforms soon wears off when recruits discover they have to

The standard Para crew cut might not be fashionable, but it serves a purpose: everyone looks the same and is treated in the same way.

iron them every day. In the opinion of one senior officer at the Depot: "Personally, I think they are impatient, and that is part of modern life today. They want to be a parachutist immediately and can hardly wait two or three weeks, and so you have to maintain the momentum all the way through."

It is not just the impatience of the recruits that strikes the Recruit Company staff. Before they join, many recruits have little knowledge of the Regiment and the training process. Some expect to be parachuting in the first week; others expect to be off to some sunny foreign country as soon as they join the Regiment. The most

Recruits wait to tackle the obstacle course. They will spend 12 weeks training for the dreaded "P" Company selection test.

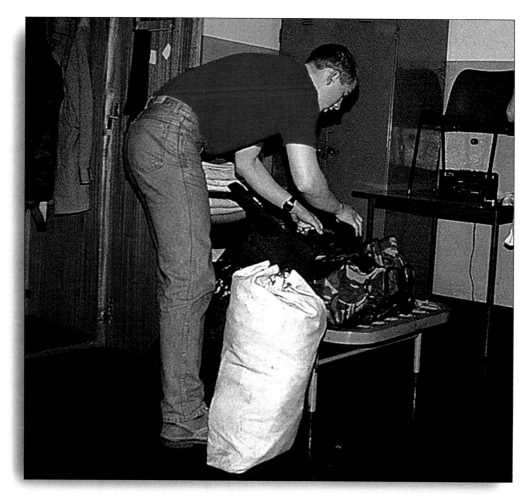

Looking after yourself means more than knowing how to fight. High standards also apply to the cleaning of accommodations.

entertaining surprise for the instructors comes at the end of Week One. They tell the recruits to pack their **bergens** (the standard backpack of the British Army) for a night of sleeping outside. Even the most experienced corporals never cease to be amazed by the slippers, pyjamas, and pillows that appear that evening. Only by sheer hard work, patience, and time do the staff succeed in turning such raw civilians into soldiers.

Push-ups, the curse of every soldier around the world. The scientific name for this type of exercise is "calisthenics," which are the parade-ground exercises designed to promote straight backs.

The first four weeks of training are taken up with the core subjects any recruit is taught on joining the British Army. These are drill (how to march on the parade ground), weapons training, who to salute and who not to salute, what each badge means, and what to call the different ranks. The recruit is also taught the history of the Regiment since the Airborne Forces were formed in 1940. This includes the important dates, people, and places. These history lessons are important. It is essential to show the recruit what airborne soldiers have achieved in the past and what they are expected to be capable of in the future. It helps to make the soldiers want to join the Regiment, to pass through all their recruit training and the fearsome "P" Company.

FIRST MISSIONS

The Paras were only a few months old when they conducted their first combat missions. One of the earliest was called Operation Biting in World War II. This was a daring raid against German positions on the French coast in 1942. A group of Paras called "C" Company 2 PARA captured a top secret radar set and two German radar experts. They did this despite having barely finished parachute training. They also had to cope with numerous enemy positions, including machine guns and artillery positions. This amazing action illustrates the courage and resourcefulness of the Paras.

Soldiers from the newly formed Parachute Regiment land at Arnhem, Holland, in September 1944. The scene of terrible fighting, it set the battle standard all Paras must meet.

TEAMWORK AND TOUGHENING UP

For a recruit, life at the Depot is very hard. Each day seems to last forever, except Sunday, the rest day, which is over in a flash. On the other days, there is very little time to relax.

A typical day at Depot begins at 0700 hours and lasts until 2200 hours. In this 15-hour period the recruit will always be busy. The pressure on the recruit is intense and constant. What spare time the recruit has is spent cleaning the barracks, polishing boots, and washing and ironing clothing or uniform. On top of the mental stress comes the physical stress of harder fitness training. The build-up to "P" Company can now begin. The runs start to get longer and longer. The recruits have to give maximum effort—not just for 10 minutes, but for 40 or 50.

As the Depot staff struggle to improve the fitness of the recruits, their biggest battle is with the modern way of life. If you are not used to hot and cold running water and a warm house, living in the field does not seem that uncomfortable. Also, if you have accepted discipline from parents, schoolteachers, and employers, then it is much easier to accept discipline from corporals and sergeant-majors. However, many young recruits show a lack of discipline when they arrive. This means that today's recruits get more of a shock when

Recruits are often so muddy by the end of the assault course that they are identifiable only by the number on their helmets.

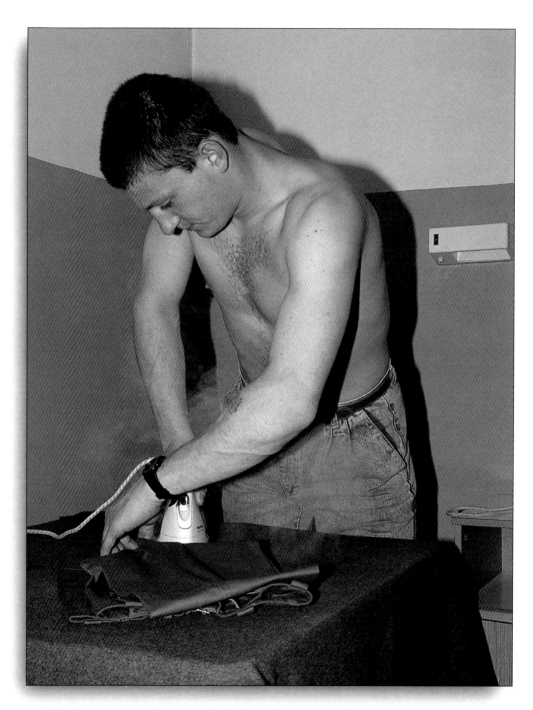

Soldiering is not all about fighting. Each recruit must become accustomed to everyday tasks, such as ironing and caring for their equipment, in order to be accepted into the Regiment.

they join the army than did their fathers or grandfathers. But if recruits really want to join the Regiment (and for the right reasons), then they will change his way of life.

What is more difficult for the instructors is that many recruits are very unfit. Many have not been involved with sports and have eaten junk food for years. Today's recruit has to work a lot harder than the soldiers of earlier generations to come up to the standards of the Parachute Regiment. The only way to survive is through teamwork. Team spirit within the **section** quickly builds up because all the recruits are going through a difficult experience together. And, because they are together for so much of the day (they live in eight-person rooms), and under pressure for most of the time, they soon get to know each other really well. The Depot staff also encourage

Physical training includes carrying exercises. Paras may have to do this for real in combat situations when rescuing injured comrades.

team spirit through competition between sections. By telling each section how it compares with the others in the platoon, they help both to bind the section together and to improve the performance of the recruits.

However, the most important function of a good team spirit is in making the recruits want to stay in training and overcome all the hurdles along the way, together with their team. Of course, if they do not fit in with the rest of the section, and pull their weight as members of the team, then they begin to feel that they do not belong, either in the section or in the Regiment. If the rest of the section enjoys a good team spirit, then they feel even more like an outsider. Such recruits are much more likely to give up when the pressure is on. A good team spirit within the section can also help recruits in a more direct way. If they are struggling at anytime—such as when they are on a run—the other members of the section will help them out or encourage them. If they are always in need of help, however, they will be unable to help out others when they need it.

Sooner or later, almost all recruits go through a bad patch in their training. Nothing seems to be going right, the pressure of Depot is getting to be too much, and depression is creeping in. It is then that a section with a good spirit will cheer up and encourage their downhearted friends to continue. But in the end, it is only the recruits themselves who can stop themselves from failing. This is very important. Behind enemy lines, often with danger and death all around them, the paratroopers need to be able to take disaster after disaster in their stride, to face each one, and then carry on fighting to achieve the mission.

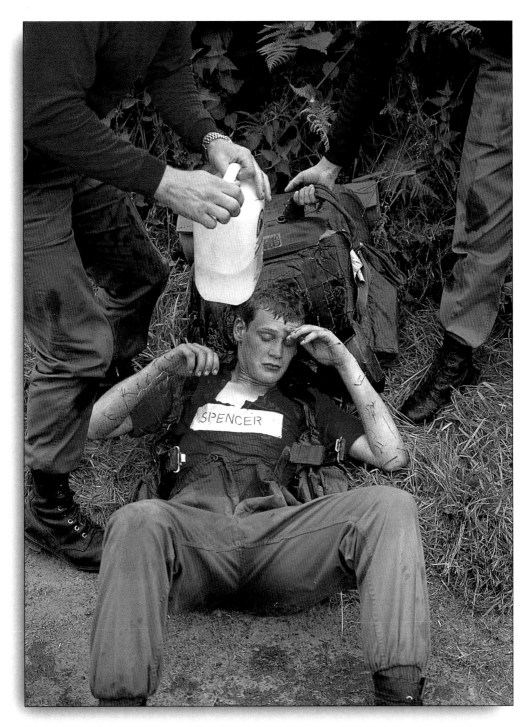

The "10-miler" is one of the punishing tests of "P" Company. This cross-country march must be completed in 1 hour 45 minutes.

Kit inspections are often a good test of whether or not the recruits are trying hard. They have to iron their uniforms carefully, including the items they are not wearing, and arrange everything neatly in the locker. Then the platoon sergeant will arrive. He will start throwing things around, and shouting at the recruits for the smallest mistake or lack of effort. If the kits are dirty or unironed, this will tell the sergeant that the recruits are no longer trying their best. It might seem a small thing to pick on, but if the soldiers cannot discipline themselves in training, they will probably not discipline themselves on the battlefield.

If recruits are struggling with training, then the Parachute Regiment has a system to help them. Once every few weeks, the platoon staff meet to talk about how the recruits are coping with the course. The officers and trainers discuss all recruits to decide which ones should not continue on the course. If recruits are not good enough, they have to go through that section of the training again. This is dreaded by the recruits, not only because of the extra time they will have to

Recruits will be punished if they fail the sergeant's inspections.

spend at Depot or the frustration of having to repeat the lessons, but also because they are separated from their friends in their section and platoon. They will have to fit into a totally new group with its own spirit, make new friends, and gain the trust of that group.

At the end of Week Four, the recruits are ready to show off what they have learned on the parade ground. This is a test of their drill, their appearance, and also their knowledge of the Parachute Regiment, past and present. With this first stage in their training completed, they are starting to show the first signs of thinking—and acting—like soldiers. Their confidence is growing, and they are working better as a team—the section and platoon spirit is getting stronger. Or it should be.

THE D-DAY LANDINGS

When the Allies landed a massive force into German-occupied Europe on June 6, 1944, the Paras had already been fighting for many hours. One of their most famous actions was against the Merville Battery. This was a German position surrounded by minefields and barbed wire. The Germans also had many machine guns and heavy artillery weapons, and numbered some 200 men. Despite this, 150 Paras with only one machine gun between them stormed the position. Nearly half the Paras were killed in this battle, but they eventually captured the position. Only 20 German soldiers survived, showing that the Paras were truly an enemy to be feared.

"P" COMPANY

The first few weeks for the recruit may have seemed tough, but they are nothing compared to what is to come. Soon the recruits will be pushing their bodies to the absolute limit of their endurance, and trying to prove that they will be good Paras.

After about four weeks, the recruits are usually given a leave for the weekend—the first time they are allowed off camp since they arrived. Nevertheless, most recruits, though glad of the break, are eager to continue with the course, because the next phase is about "real" training. This involves exercises in the field and shooting on the ranges. And real soldiering is the reason they all joined.

Part of this period of "individual training," is spent near Brecon, Wales (a small country within the United Kingdom), and it is known as "Basic Wales." The recruits learn how to camouflage themselves, how to move without being seen or heard, how to judge the distance to a target, and all the other basic skills a soldier must master before he or she can become a Para. Basic Wales also involves three days of adventure training. As well as building up the recruits' characters, the 17-mile (27-km) marches introduce them to the hills that they will come to know very well during "P" Company. Once back from Wales, the recruits spend some more time at Aldershot on basic skills and shooting. Then comes the big

"P" Company is designed to push recruits to their physical limits. The Steeplechase course must be completed in 17.5 minutes.

test itself—the two and a half weeks of "P" Company. Not until the recruits have passed "P" Company do they receive the red beret.

The first hurdle to overcome is the called the "Steeplechase." This is a four-fifths of a mile (1.3-km) course run in woods near the barracks. The recruits run around this twice in their boots, shorts, and training tops. It takes an average of 17.5 minutes of determined effort, struggling through water jumps, fighting through mud, and clambering over the obstacles scattered along the route.

This grand start to "P" Company begins with all the recruits lying on their stomachs in a line in the middle of the playing fields next to the woods. When a **Thunderflash** (a loud hand grenade) goes off behind them, everyone leaps to their feet and sprints toward the trees and the first obstacle. The Steeplechase is

The Steeplechase must be done at maximum speed. The two laps of the four-fifths of a mile (1.3-km) course leave the recruits exhausted.

a race against the clock—a test of how fit the recruits really are. They have to run through ditches of freezing filthy water, climb over assault courses, and climb over high wooden walls. Each soldier tries to beat the others. If they begin to slow down half-way through the second lap, there is nothing that will speed them more than the sound of panting and splashing behind them, and the recruits fight even harder to avoid being overtaken. With the Steeplechase over, the recruits—still panting and covered in mud and leaves from head to foot—return to barracks to prepare quickly for the next event: the Log Race.

This is a test not only of fitness but also of teamwork. It is designed to find out whether recruits will be strong when the going gets tough, and whether they will push themselves to their limits rather than let down their mates. Designed to represent dragging a WOMBAT 120-mm antitank gun into action, teams of about eight people run around a one-and-three-quarters–mile (2.8-km) course, carrying a log the size of a telegraph pole which weighs approximately 655 pounds (295 kg). Each team sets out to win.

The course lasts for only 13 minutes, but it seems like forever. It is 13 minutes of hell. The flat parts of the course are sand, so it is just like trying to run on a soft beach. As if this were not bad enough, halfway round is what seems to be a nearly vertical hill. Struggling up this, the recruits really start to feel the weight of the log. It is like running on loose stones—for every step they take up, the soldiers seem to slip back two. But, though their lungs are gasping for air, and their bodies are begging them to stop, the recruits have to keep going. If they drop off the log and do not get

The Log Race is another grueling test. It is designed to simulate carrying a heavy 120-mm antitank gun into action.

straight back on, they let down all their comrades—with whom they may have trained for the last 12 weeks—since a team that is one person short stands much less chance of winning. Also, by dropping off the log, they immediately fail "P" Company. Once on the flat again, it is back to running on sand. Somehow, the sight of the rival log and the finishing line just ahead gives the recruits a bit of extra energy. Once they are across the finishing line, the recruits know that they have passed the first two events of "P" Company.

That afternoon comes "milling"—a test, not of fitness or strength, but of pure aggression. The word milling is derived from mill or to grind grain, meaning hard work. Wearing 16-ounce (454-g) boxing gloves, the recruit has to stand toe-to-toe with another recruit and box for a minute. It is not true boxing, however; no dodging, weaving, or guarding is allowed—it is a test of how much punishment the recruit can give and take. The recruits who have fought already, or are waiting to fight, sit in their teams around the ring. Every time a recruit lands a good punch, a mighty cheer goes up; every time an opponent lands one, the opposing team roars. It lasts only a minute, but it seems like the longest minute in the world.

With the milling over, the recruits are allowed to go home for the weekend to prepare themselves for the coming week of tough exercises. What they need to do in the last few days before the long endurance tests of "P" Company is eat and sleep. Monday

"Milling" tests aggression and determination. The recruits must box flat out for one minute, giving and taking as many punches as they can.

The "10-Miler" must be carried out with a full backpack, weighing around 48 lb (22 kg), and the British Army SA80 rifle. The recruit must finish in one hour and 45 minutes.

morning begins with the "10-Miler," a classic Parachute Regiment speed march. The 10-Miler (16 km) tests the recruits to see if they can cover long distances quickly. The recruits run this test carrying nearly 48 pounds (22 kg) of kit and rifle and must finish it in an hour and 45 minutes.

Although it starts off on smooth roads, it soon starts going cross-country, and before long the recruits are scrambling up steep, pebble covered hills. Past the halfway mark and they are once again running on sand. However, this stretch is also used regularly as a training area for tanks. This leaves the heavy sand all churned up. Therefore, it is not only more tiring but also more dangerous. But it is not all running. About half is running (known as "**doubling**," from "double quick time"), and half is marching—though marching at such a pace that it is almost as fast as running.

Just after halfway, the recruits are starting to feel the pain. It is getting harder and harder to persuade their bodies to keep going at the speed they know they must. When they are doubling, the recruits can hardly wait for the order to march. They know that at any moment they are going to hear it, but they must keep pushing their bodies for that little bit longer until they do. They cannot afford to drop out of the squad. Then at last the order comes.

But now the recruits find that they really have to open up the pace, to move their legs quickly and swing their arms in order to keep going quickly. It seems as though quick time is not much slower than double time. All that seems to change is that it is a different leg muscle that they are pushing to the limit. After a few more paces, they cannot wait to hear the order to break into double-quick time again.

Blisters are a problem during the long marches. Medics administer doses of "Tincbenco," a medicine to draw out blisters.

TRAINING PAYS OFF

The Falklands War showed how important hard training really is. It was the tough, thorough training of its carefully chosen soldiers that helped the Red Berets to win some of the hardest battles of the war. Soldiers have said that they were surprised at how similar battle was to training. Some Paras walked almost 30 miles (48 km) across the island and went straight into battle at the end of it. Most of the men carried over 70 pounds (32 kg) of pack and some over 100 pounds (45 kg). Such enormous weights could not have been taken into battle had not the soldiers been through the training of something like "P" Company. The biggest difference from training, however, was that the enemy was firing real bullets, not the blanks fired by Para instructors. Despite this, most Paras overcame their fear and showed amazing courage in battle.

But, no matter how much it hurts, no matter how much effort it takes to keep going, the soldiers cannot afford to complain, even in their minds. Because, if they do, they will find themselves dropping behind, too far behind to catch up. And it is important to stay with the squad. Even if they are at the back, the others will help drag each other along. When they at last reach the end of the 10-Miler, the recruits are absolutely exhausted. But they do not have long to rest, because it is straight on to the "**Trainasium.**"

THE "TRAINASIUM" AND FINAL FITNESS CHALLENGES

The Trainasium is a course set within the grounds of the Depot. Its aim is to put the recruit under mental pressure, and to test if the recruit is courageous enough to jump out of a balloon or an airplane.

One part of the Trainasium is about 22 feet (7 m) above the ground. The recruit has to run along a catwalk only one foot (30 cm) wide, leap gaps, crawl along two wires about a shoulder width apart, and other such tests of confidence and nerve. The second part includes the "high shuffle bars" and the "standing jump."

The high shuffle bars are two poles, set a shoulder width apart and about 49 feet (15 m) above the ground. With nothing to hang on to, recruits shuffle the 13 feet (4 m) to the end of the poles. Just before they reach the end, an instructor on the ground orders the recruits to stop, bend down, and touch their toes, so they have to see how high up they are.

Beneath the high shuffle bars are two platforms. One is about six and a half feet (2 m) below the poles, and about as wide as the gap between them. The recruits can only see it if they look straight down between their legs. The other is a much larger platform, 20 feet (6 m) below the bars.

The Trainasium tests the recruits' nerve. Even worse, it must be completed soon after the "10-Miler" has already caused wobbly legs.

Although the high shuffle bars cause the greatest fear for most recruits, it is the standing jump that causes most to fail. The recruits climb onto a platform about 13 feet (4 m) above the ground, and when an instructor shouts "Go!" they have to leap across a gap to another platform, about eight feet (2.5 m) away. As the recruits move forward to the edge, it seems an impossible distance to cross from a standing jump. But it is not, as the instructor has proved only minutes beforehand.

On all the Trainasium tests, the recruits are given three chances. The instructor will give the order three times. If the recruits have

Touching your toes might seem easy, but trying it 49 feet (15 m) above the ground while balancing on two poles is a different matter.

Soldiers prepare themselves while waiting to go on the Trainasium. The recruits are given three chances to complete all sections of this test.

Recruits must conquer the Brecon Beacons mountains. The weather can change very quickly from 80°F (27°C) to less than 32°F (0°C).

Recruits are under constant assessment. Every test is designed to simulate the mental and physical endurance necessary for combat.

still not reacted after the third, they fail "P" Company, no matter how well they have done on any of the other tests. What it takes to pass the Trainasium is the ability to overcome fear. The mental pressure comes because the Trainasium is high enough that if you did fall off, you would certainly be injured.

Even when they have completed the Trainasium tests, the recruits have little time to relax. Before long, they are back up in the woods where they did the Steeplechase, and back on the Assault Course. The course is a 440-yard (400-m) circuit with 18 obstacles. The recruits have to go around three times. After this, the recruits return

The Stretcher Race simulates carrying a wounded comrade. Recruits must carry a 165-pound (75-kg) stretcher for seven miles (12 km).

to barracks. There, they prepare for the move back to Wales for an exercise called Steel Bayonet—two and a half days in the Brecon Beacons mountains, with everyone living in the field.

On the first day, the recruits have to march 17 miles (27 km), carrying a weapon, bergen, and all the clothing and rations required for two days' survival. The aim is to tire out the recruits and to give them confidence in their ability to cover long distances with a heavy load, which weighs about 48 pounds (22 kg).

The second day begins with a nine-and-a-third–mile (15-km) march over the peaks of Pen-y-Fan and Fan Fawr. At first, the going is fairly easy, up a slope that is not too steep. But it gradually gets worse, changing first to bricks set at all angles, and then just to mud. And the last 545 yards (500 m) up to Pen-y-Fan is an almost vertical slope. This is a real test after three and three-quarters miles (6 km) of uphill walking with 48 pounds (22 kg) on your back. And the final 328 feet (100 m) is so steep the recruits use handholds to climb it.

After going along a ridge, then down into a valley and up again to Fan Fawr, the platoon stops for lunch. But the break is short, and no sooner have the recruits sat down, than they are off again for a six-and-a-quarter–mile (10-km) speed march, to be completed in an hour and eight minutes.

After a second night in the field, the recruits have to face the final test of "P" Company—the Stretcher Race. This is one of the most difficult events. Teams of about 12 persons race against each other over seven miles (12 km) of grinding hills. It is designed to be similar to carrying a wounded comrade off the battlefield, with four people carrying the specially weighted stretcher while the others take the team's weapons. Every so often, two recruits on the stretcher change over. Swapping weapons, people, and a moving stretcher takes good teamwork to get it right. For the recruit, just keeping going is painful. But once on the stretcher, the soldiers also get their share of the pain of 165 pounds (75 kg) of metal stretcher bouncing up and down on their raw shoulders.

For about an hour and 20 minutes, they have to survive it, to give everything for the team to win. If they drop too far behind the stretcher, or refuse to go on it when ordered to change, then they fail. They have let their team down and they must work that much harder to stay in the race. After crossing the finishing line, the recruits can rest their aching legs and shoulders and let their bodies recover. A mug of warm sweet tea has never tasted so good. Now the recruits wait to see if they have passed "P" Company. Officially, the recruits will have to wait to be told if they have passed. But they have a good idea of how well they have done. The sense of achievement when you know you have passed is amazing.

So what is it that makes someone pass or fail? Certainly, one major reason for failing is injury—broken feet or sprained ankles are common in training. As well, a recruit has to join for the right reasons, not simply to escape problems at home. The sort of person who passes is, according to one officer at Depot: "The quieter, more self-reliant person with above average intelligence. He is quick-witted and sharp. He may not be academically intellectual, but he's certainly no fool. And it's that sort of character, a well-rounded young man, that makes it. The rather brazen and flashy sort of character—he doesn't make it."

But intelligence is not the only quality needed to pass "P" Company itself. What is also required is strength of character. Airborne soldiers are certainly fit, but they are no superheroes. The soldiers feel fear and pain. But, crucially, they can force themselves to overcome these feelings. It is, in the end, "all in the mind." The recruits' first reward for passing "P" Company is that they are now allowed to wear the red beret.

TIPS FOR COMPLETING THE TRAINASIUM

The Trainasium is one of the most feared sections of training for the Parachute Regiment. However, though recruits have been injured by falling off, the Trainasium is as mentally challenging as it is physically demanding. There are several important points about completing it successfully. The first is to use your imagination. If the Trainasium was only a few feet off the ground, then it would be easy to complete. This means that it is simply fear that is making it difficult. Some soldiers actually try to imagine that the ground is just beneath them. If they can keep this thought, they can do the course much more easily. The other skill is not to think too hard about what you are doing. The instructors are looking for someone who does not hesitate. Therefore, doing the course quickly, without stopping to think of the danger, not only helps you to get over it but also helps you get the instructor's approval.

PARACHUTE TRAINING AND THE BALLOON JUMP

Next, the Paras go on to parachute training at the Royal Air Force base at Brize Norton. Here, they must listen and learn, or they could suffer serious injury. And before every jump, the soldiers must overcome their natural fear of jumping into thin air.

The basic parachuting course is called **Basic Para**. Basic Para lasts for four weeks and takes place at No. 1 Parachute Training School (No. 1 PTS) located at RAF Brize Norton in Oxfordshire. The Training is actually done by the Royal Air Force Parachute Jump Instructors (**PJIs**). Those at Brize Norton train all the British Armed Forces' parachutists. Trainees on Basic Para are divided up into groups of seven or eight people. The trainee Paras are kept together. Each group has its own PJI, who stays with the recruits for the full four weeks.

First, the recruits are taught how to land correctly. Much attention is paid to mastering this skill—it could mean the difference between hitting the ground ready to fight, and breaking a leg before the fighting has even started. Because of this, the first period of almost every day of the course is given over to landing practice. And not only landing from the front. The British service parachute cannot be steered. That means the soldiers have no control over the direction of their landing. They must be taught how to land backward and from

Parachute training involves using the flight swing. This is a harness used to practice controlling the parachute canopy during descent.

Paras must jump in tight patterns. A C-130 Hercules plane can take up to 90 paratroopers, who must jump in close succession.

the side, as well as from the front. In a 40-minute period, each student will perform between 20 and 30 parachute rolls from any angle the instructor shouts out.

For the first three days, all training is designed around the first real parachute test—jumping from a balloon. After that, the students are taught how to jump from an aircraft. They are dressed as they would be for the real thing and taken aboard a realistic mock-up of a **Hercules** aircraft. Here they get their first taste of waiting for the green light to come on, which tells them that they have to jump.

The recruits are given one session jumping from these "mock doors," as they are known, and then go on to the **Fan Exit Trainer**. This is also a mock-up aircraft, but as the trainees jump out (without parachutes), a giant fan blasts them with air so that they

Learning how to land safely is a vital skill. Feet and knees must be together, with elbows tucked in, close to the body.

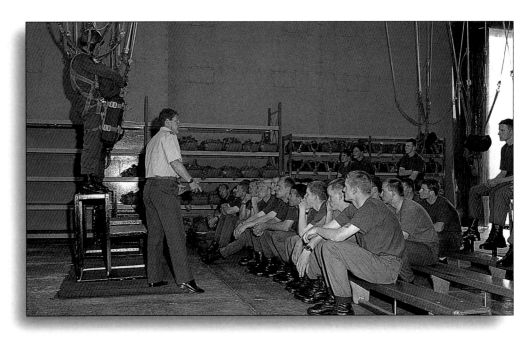

As well as practical exercises, the Paras' training course involves how and why parachutes work. Two different types of parachutes are used, the PX-5 and the PX-4.

know what it will be like to jump into the **slipstream** of a speeding aircraft. Early on in the first week, this piece of equipment is used purely for jump training. But as the week goes on, it is also used for landing practice. In addition, the heights from which landings are attempted gradually increase as the course builds up to the balloon jump.

A jump from a 70-foot (21-m) tower takes place on the Wednesday of the first week. On the same day, the trainees are introduced to the parachutes that they will use for their first jump from a balloon (known as a "**balloon-car descent**"). All week they have been practicing. By Thursday morning, they are as ready as they will ever be for the descent itself.

The balloon-car descent has long struck fear into the hearts of those who are about to do it. Almost from the moment they pass through the gates of Depot, recruits are told horror stories of how terrifying the balloon jump is. It is often regarded as being worse than exiting from a low-flying aircraft. This is because the recruit is surrounded by the eerie silence of a balloon cage hanging and swaying in midair. There is no engine noise, no wind, no slipstream —just the rocking motions of the cage. The absence of slipstream also means that you feel yourself dropping like a stone, rather than being buffeted by turbulence.

Four trainees at a time accompany their PJI in the balloon cage as it rises to 800 feet (243 m) above the training DZ. Nerves are taut,

With 20 minutes to go to the drop point, recruits stand up and hook their lines to the wire that will automatically release the parachute.

and many recruits will tell jokes to try to relieve the tension. But some of these trips are silent, because people are too nervous to speak, let alone make up a joke.

The balloon is tied to the ground by a long line. As the line connecting the cage with the ground tautens, the PJI draws back the bar blocking the exit. The first candidate steps forward to stand tensely in the door. Once certain everything is right for the parachute jump, the instructor screams "Go!" and the trainee is gone, plummeting earthward. After 200 feet (60 m), the fall is slowed down as the parachute opens. It only remains for the recruit to steer into open space and perform a good landing.

Although the balloon descent is not something many want to repeat, some people feel that the jump is not as bad as others claim. A trainee who had recently completed his balloon jump, said this about it:

"It was all right; not as bad as everyone in the unit said it would be. Everyone says you drop like a stone, and get this big jerk on your back. But in our balloon cage, the recruits went up, backed me up, had a bit of a joke on the way up to relieve our nerves. It's really unnerving looking out. I looked over the side and thought, 'This is a bit further than I thought it would be.' But when it came to going out, it was all right. I was the last man out; all the other lads had gone, and I thought, 'I'm not going to let them down and myself down,' and it was all right. And as for this big drop—within no time at all the parachute was open. I had a really big smile from one ear to the other, and the feeling of having done something completely different from anything I'd experienced before."

THE BIRTH OF THE WORLD'S PARAS

The first parachute-trained soldiers were created in Italy in 1928. Two years later, the Soviet Union formed a parachute battalion and in 1937 the first French para unit was formed. In April 1940, Germany unleashed its own parachute force on Norway and then, in May, on the Netherlands. The success of these operations convinced the British Prime Minister Winston Churchill that the Allies should have their own parachute troops. Churchill was so impressed that he called for the creation of a 5,000-man parachute unit. Training began. Many other nations quickly followed the British example, and today most nations have their own airborne troops.

Nevertheless, some people just cannot do the jump—fear overcomes them and they freeze to the spot. It has been known for a Para to go on and quite happily complete actual parachute jumps from aircraft, and then freeze in the door when asked to jump from the balloon. Those who do refuse are sent away—they have failed to make it as Paras. The removal is done quietly with the minimum of fuss, and the recruits who refuse are not allowed any contact with their former colleagues for fear of what effect they may have on the others' performance over the rest of the course. But it is very rare for people to refuse to jump.

For those who successfully do their balloon jump, the program goes on to let them jump from aircraft, the true method of the Para.

THE FINAL JUMPS

Once he or she has done the balloon jump, the trainee needs to do only eight jumps from an aircraft to become a full member of the Parachute Regiment and one of the world's elite soldiers.

A slide show and lecture on jumping from an aircraft takes up Monday afternoon of the second week. This is known as "**aircraft drill**." Aircraft drill continues through Tuesday. Then the students are taken up in a C-130 Hercules transport aircraft. This is simply to get them used to the aircraft and what they should expect.

Wednesday brings the Paras' first encounter with the **Outdoor Exit Trainer**. This 40-foot (12-m) tower is designed to simulate what it is like to exit into the roaring slipstream of an aircraft. Cables are hooked up to the Paras and these pull them as soon as they jump out of the door. These cables then carry the Paras for about 320 feet (106 m). The Outdoor Exit Trainer is also used to teach and test the students on what to do if they land in water. This includes how to hit the water softly and how to get their parachutes off their backs—if they do not, the parachutes will pull them underwater. This is the last step in the training before they actually take to the skies and do their first parachute jump from an aircraft.

Exactly a week after they drifted to 800 feet (243 m) in the balloon cage, the trainees find themselves sitting in the fuselage of a

The light at the top right of the door goes green, indicating "Go!" Kit can sometimes be so heavy, Paras must be pushed out of the door.

The C–130 Hercules aircraft is the workhorse of the Parachute Regiment. It not only carries Paras, but can also handle tanks, jeeps, trucks, and helicopters.

C–130 Hercules. This time it is for real. The first time they jump, it is without equipment from 1,000 feet (330 m). The absence of containers and weapons makes the aircraft less cluttered, and the Paras can walk more easily to the door because there is nothing to trip over. The routine is exactly the same as it has been in all the practice rounds jumps. Approaching the DZ, each soldier stands up and hooks up the **static line** to the rail running along the side of the fuselage. When the red light goes on, the first soldier stands in the door. When the green light comes on, go!

Once through the slipstream, the Paras fall a short way before their parachutes open. They have passed the first big hurdle. But now, the Paras' attention must focus on the coming landing. An experienced Para tells us what goes through his mind as he heads toward the ground: "You get nervous when you are actually going to hit the ground, especially if you are traveling fast. Then the nerves makes your body go stiff. You can see the ground coming toward you. All you can think is, 'Oh, well. Here we go.' "

The first descent is done with six people jumping out each time the aircraft passes over the DZ. But the second and third jumps, which take place during Week Three, are more complicated. In the second, the Paras leap from both sides of the aircraft at almost exactly the same moment. In the third, a large number of Paras jump together.

The winged Para badge is what every recruit wants to wear. The tartan element on this badge indicates that it belongs to a member of the Territorial Army (TA), Britain's volunteer armed forces.

This gives the Paras an insight into what an actual battle jump might be like.

From Thursday afternoon onward, training is dedicated to jumping with equipment. Jumping from an aircraft carrying over 100 pounds (45 kg) of weapons and kit truly separates the paratrooper from the sports parachutist. Everything that the trainees have learned up to now is repeated again, but this time carrying a rifle and a bergen that is packed with a soldier's essentials. Jumping with all this extra weight and bulk needs a huge amount of fitness and stamina.

Flying with equipment all around is an uncomfortable business. Because the parachute is on the soldier's back, the bergen is attached to hooks at the front so that it hangs down over the tops of the legs. When the command to stand up is given, the Paras have to struggle to their feet. They might have to stand upright with all this weight for as long as 20 minutes. After all this, going through the door comes as a relief.

Once he is out the door, the Para checks that their main **canopies** (the material in their parachutes) have opened properly. Then they flick catches on both the hooks securing the bergen. The bergen then drops away beneath them on a line 16 feet (5 m) long. This means that the heavy equipment hits the ground before the Paras land. Nevertheless, the first thing that the trainees notice when they try this in training is that their landings are heavier. Many Paras get twisted ankles and knees on landing. Sometimes even worse accidents can happen, but the Paras accept this as part of training to be elite soldiers—danger is always involved.

Descending and landing close together can present problems. With lots of parachutes so close to each other, ones nearer to the ground can "steal" the air of canopies above them, causing them to collapse.

The Paras have to do three parachute jumps with equipment. Each jump gets more and more difficult. Not only do the Paras have to do their own jumps well, they must also coordinate themselves with all the others who are jumping at the same time. If they can do all these jumps properly, then the trainees can finally become fully qualified Paras. But the course is not over yet. There is still an operational parachute jump to make. This is a drop that is made as close as possible to a real parachute jump into battle. Thursday morning of the fourth week is spent in preparation, going through

Recruits try to catch some sleep, but jumping is very hard work. Containers can weigh from 120 pounds (54 kg) to 180 pounds (80 kg).

operational aircraft drills and then making sure that everything is in its correct place on the aircraft. In the afternoon, the Paras take off for the DZ.

It is during this jump that the newly qualified Paras come the closest so far to experiencing what actually happens in a combat **airdrop**. As the aircraft approaches the DZ, chaos reigns aboard as everyone struggles with their kit in the confined space. One instructor here describes what goes on. Remember, he is talking about veterans, not trainees: "Sometimes I feel so sorry for the blokes [men]. They have to fly around for two hours at low level with the aircraft ducking and weaving. They start being sick everywhere."

This is what a Para himself has to say about the experience: "From the time the green light goes on, you want to jump. Your eyes are locked on the light, and you go—nobody can stop you; and if they did try to do so, there would probably be a fight. When you do jump, you really want to because you have been standing there for ages, frightened—or nervous, certainly. After the waiting, you need to jump, and there is nothing worse than getting ready for it and then being told: 'Stop!'

"You are very tired after all the stress of waiting and then actually jumping. You've done seven hours' work getting everything ready before you even make the jump. You are really wound-up emotionally. You can feel the atmosphere in the plane; being with 90 guys in a Hercules with full equipment is hard work. There are different characters, of course. Some sit and go to sleep automatically. As soon as they get on the aircraft, they sit there and snooze. But then, other people enjoy having a good talk.

"Busy drops are the worst, because the aircraft is full of people and equipment. Different soldiers have different roles and the containers they carry vary from 120 pounds (54 kg) to about 180 pounds (80 kg) in weight. These huge things are crammed into a really small space and you have guys falling over each other trying to stand up and move around. Then you have a dispatcher trying to do his checks and walking all over everybody. It's chaos—but it works. It's easy parachuting when there is hardly anyone in the aircraft and no containers and so on, but when it is full it is very hard work."

Most elite units train their soldiers in parachute techniques. At the very least, this means training the soldiers to do what are

A "static line" drop opens parachutes automatically at low altitudes. Paras can also "freefall" from 32,000 feet (10,000 m).

known as "static line" drops. Here a large number of troops jump from a transport aircraft and their parachutes open automatically. Yet this method is slow and it leaves the transport aircraft vulnerable to being shot down. That is why some new methods of parachuting have been designed.

A more speedy and secret way of putting soldiers behind enemy lines from the air is called High-Altitude, Low-Opening (HALO) parachuting. In this case, the troops jump from the aircraft at an altitude of 32,000 feet (10,000 m). They do not open their parachutes straight away. Instead, they freefall to an altitude of about 2,500 feet

TYPES OF PARACHUTE JUMP

There are two main types of parachute jump—static line and freefall. All parachutes are pulled out of their packs by something called a ripcord. In Static Line, the ripcord is attached by a cable to the inside of the aircraft. When the Para jumps out, the cable unravels. At a safe distance from the aircraft, the cable goes taut and pulls the ripcord. This in turn pulls the parachute out. Static line jumps have the advantage that everybody's parachute opens at the right height and there is less room for mistakes. Freefall parachuting means that the Paras have no static line and simply fall through the air until they pull the ripcord with their own hands. Freefall is much more dangerous and is usually used only by elite units for dropping behind enemy lines.

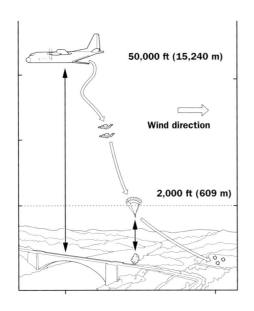

50,000 ft (15,240 m)

Wind direction

2,000 ft (609 m)

HALO Paras "freefall" first, then open their chutes at 2,500 feet (800 m).

(800 m), when they open their parachute. This means that they get from the aircraft to the ground very quickly, which in turn means they are less likely to be spotted.

However, this type of parachuting requires a great deal of training. Freefallers, for example, have to keep stable positions during the flight wearing heavy backpacks and their weapons strapped to their bodies by harnesses. At high altitudes, HALO jumpers also need oxygen-breathing equipment—there is not enough air to breathe at 10,000 feet (3,000 m). They are falling so fast that they need a special machine called a "barometric trigger" to open their parachutes automatically at the right altitude. If they leave it until too late, they could hit the ground before their parachutes have opened properly.

In addition, the paratroopers will be exposed to freezing temperatures as they freefall. This may result in ice forming on their equipment, especially their goggles. These problems mean that HALO jumpers need to be in prime physical shape and highly skilled, both of which require a great deal of time and training. As a result, only the best elite units, such as the SAS units, U.S. Special Forces, and the SEALs train their recruits in HALO parachuting techniques.

HAHO parachuting is different from HALO parachuting. HAHO stands for High-Altitude, High-Opening. The paratroopers are dropped from the aircraft wearing oxygen-breathing equipment at an altitude of 32,000 feet (10,000 m). However, they freefall for only 8 to 10 seconds and then open the parachute at around 27,600 feet (8,500 m). They then slowly, silently, float to the ground. This can take between 70 and 80 minutes, by which time they will have traveled up to 19 miles (30 km). This means the team can be dropped outside enemy territory, and then drift behind enemy lines unseen by radar.

But there are problems with HAHO parachuting. The team must stay together once the parachutes are opened to be sure of landing together. This can be very difficult because winds can scatter people for miles. All the soldiers must be experts at "flying" their parachutes if they are to land together.

For the operational jump, groups of 15—or even 20—jump at once from a height of around 800 feet (243 m). This really is the final descent of the course, and as the recruits are driven back to Brize Norton, they know that all they have to do now is hand back their equipment, and the parachute wings will be theirs. Yet for all that they have been through, the Para squad has not finished training yet. The pass-out parade remains.

HAHO Paras "fly" to their targets from a high altitude.

FINALLY A PARA

After passing the tough selection course, the new Paras join their chosen family, the Parachute Regiment. In their battalions, the recruits find a world full of challenges, one in which experienced corporals and sergeants watch their every move.

When the Paras march off the parade ground after the pass-out parade, it is one of the proudest moments of their lives. They felt a tremendous sense of achievement when they passed "P" Company, and also when they got through Basic Para. But now they have finished what they set out to do so many weeks ago, and they start to feel relief that at last it is all over, as well as satisfaction that they have finally made it. Wearing red berets, with wings on their arms, they have become proud members of the Parachute Regiment.

When the recruits go on well-earned leave, their families will notice a change in them. One sergeant-major at the Depot describes those recruits who make it to the end: "When they have finished here —oh yeah, they have certainly changed. They form a bond with the people, and their outlook on life is very different. They form a new family. Very few Paras will mix much with their old civilian friends, because they are now in a different world. They are received into the Regiment, the battalion, they have cut their family ties to a certain extent and left home."

A proud moment. The red beret is ready to be presented to a recruit who is about to become a full member of the Parachute Regiment.

For the new Para, "home" is the battalion, which is likely to be based in Montgomery Lines, directly across the road from the Depot. Despite its closeness, however, for the soldier fresh out of training it is like a world away. But it may not seem so at first. New Paras straight from Depot are reminded exactly why they did "P" Company: they are faced with having to do 10-mile runs on their very first day in battalion. And a 10-miler is a regular feature of the company training program.

The new Para joins a family of 2,000 people. And family will be the right word. Many of those in the battalion will have known each other for six or more years. This makes The Parachute Regiment a very close community. All the soldiers share a sense of pride and belonging at being a Para.

The smile says it all. At passing out parade, the newly qualified Para joins an elite group of only 2,000.

Training is over, but the Para will continue to do 10-mile (16-km) training runs and foreign tours of duty lasting several months.

A private from the Paras in the late 1990s. His SA80 rifle is fitted with a combat "SUSAT" (Sight Unit Small Arms Trilux) telescopic sight.

The new Para is posted to a section, very different from the squad in which, as a recruit, he or she passed through Depot. This section is supposed to be around eight people, but it is usually less. The new arrival soon discovers that the other members of the section will usually have been in for some time, and the relationship between the corporal commanding it and the rest is more relaxed.

Having been thrown into such a large family with all its long established groups, the new Paras have to start to make friends and to fit in with the others. Besides discovering that they have still got much to learn about soldiering, the soldiers must also adapt to the different way they are treated at Battalion. The tense atmosphere of Depot, with the pressure to pass "P" Company and get through the rest of the recruit course, is gone. However, although the atmosphere at Battalion might seem more relaxed on the surface, it demands greater maturity from the individual soldier. Rather than being told what to do all the time, the Para is required to be much more self-disciplined.

Training to be a Para is one of the toughest military programs in the world. The history of the Parachute Regiment shows us why the training has to be so difficult. The Paras have fought in every environment from the hot deserts of Africa, to the icy landscape of the Falkland Islands. In every war or conflict, they have struck terror into the hearts of their enemy through their courage and stamina. They are the type of regiment that wins battles. Whatever the future holds for the British Army, the Paras will always be there, waiting to serve their country with their elite skills.

GLOSSARY

Airborne operations The words used to describe soldiers going into battle by helicopter, aircraft, or parachute.

Aircraft drill Practicing the method of getting ready to do a parachute jump from an aircraft.

Airdrop Another name for a parachute drop of either people or equipment.

Balloon-car descent The part of Para recruits' training in which they must jump out of a hot-air balloon at a height of 800 feet (243 m).

Basic Para The shortened name for the four-week course that teaches the Para recruits how to do a parachute jump. The words stand for "Basic Parachuting."

Bergens Large backpacks used by all the soldiers of the British Army to hold their equipment.

Canopies The large pieces of material in parachutes which actually catch the air and stop parachutists from falling too fast.

Company A group of soldiers usually commanded by a major or captain.

D-Day The day in World War II—June 6, 1944—on which the Allied forces landed in German-occupied France and began to take back Europe from the Germans.

Depot Browning Barracks, Aldershot, England, where recruits to the Paras spend 12 hard weeks in basic training.

Doubling A term for a march at running pace. It comes from the expression "double-quick time."

Drills Practice exercises, such as marching on a parade ground, and also practice procedures.

DZ Drop Zone. The place where Paras are dropped during a parachute operation.

Fan Exit Trainer A mock-up aircraft that Paras use to practice parachute jumps. It has large fans that blow air at the recruits when they jump out of the door.

Hercules A very large aircraft used for transporting military equipment and vehicles, and also for dropping Paras.

Kit The equipment carried by a soldier.

NCOs This means "noncommissioned officers." It refers to soldiers who are not privates but who are not classed as officers—people such as corporals and sergeants.

Outdoor Exit Trainer A mock-up aircraft used to train recruits for making a parachute jump. The recruits are attached to long cables, and these pull them quickly sideways when they jump to imitate the slipstream of a real parachute jump.

"P" Company An incredibly tough two-and-a-half week training course which all Para recruits must endure. Long marches and exhausting obstacle courses test every person to their limit.

PJIs Parachute Jump Instructors. These are members of the RAF who teach Para recruits how to do parachute jumps.

Posthumously To receive recognition after death.

RAF Royal Air Force.

Red beret Because the Paras wear red berets, they are often called Red Berets themselves.

Section A small group of soldiers.

Slipstream When an aircraft is flying, the air rushes past the aircraft at great speed. This is called the slipstream, and it hits the Paras with enormous force when they jump from the plane.

Static line A cable that Paras attach to an aircraft and their parachutes.

Thunderflash A hand grenade that is not very dangerous but which makes an enormous flash and bang when it goes off.

Toms Soldiers in the Parachute Regiment with the rank of private.

Trainasium A piece of training equipment set high above the ground. The Paras use it to make themselves confident with heights.

Utrinque Paratus "Ready for Anything," the Parachute Regiment's motto.

Victoria Crosses The highest awards that any soldier can receive in the British Forces.

1500 hours To avoid confusion, the military measures time by the 24-hour clock. Hence, 3 P.M. becomes 1500 hours.

CHRONOLOGY

April 1940	German Paras are used for the first time in World War II in Norway, Holland, and Belgium.
June 22, 1940	Winston Churchill, the British Prime Minister, orders that a British parachute regiment should be formed with no less than 5,000 men in it. A training school is established.
February 1941	British airborne soldiers do their first combat operation. In Operation Colossus, seven officers and 31 men attack the Tragino Aqueduct in southern Italy.
February 27, 1942	British airborne soldiers launch a successful attack on a German radar station at Bruneval on the coast of France.
August 1, 1942	The Parachute Regiment is formally created.
June 5/6, 1944	Paras drop behind enemy lines in France hours before the Allied landings at Normandy—D-Day.
September 17, 1944	Huge numbers of Paras drop into the Dutch town of Arnhem in an attempt to capture German positions. The Paras are cut off from the Allied army and they suffer terrible numbers of casualties.

October 31, 1956	Paras are used by with French airborne troops in an attempt to capture the Suez Canal in Egypt.
April 1964	The Paras are used with the Royal Marine Commandos to fight guerrilla warfare and terrorism in the Middle East.
1969	The Paras begin patrols in Northern Ireland. The Regiment would keep operating there for over three decades.
April–June 1982	Paras fight some of the toughest battles of the Falklands War and win some great victories. The war costs them 40 dead and 82 wounded.
1991	Parachute Regiment forms part of U.N. forces during the Gulf War.
1999	Paras are used on peacekeeping missions in the regions of Bosnia and Kosovo.
2000–2001	Paras are sent on operational peacekeeping duties in Sierra Leone, a country torn by civil war.

RECRUITMENT INFORMATION

The Parachute Regiment takes recruits from the United Kingdom and Commonwealth countries, but also accepts some people from other nations if appropriate. All recruitment begins at an Armed Forces Careers Office—most towns and cities in England have one. Visit one of these and the army recruiting officer will tell you what you need to do. You will have to complete a simple intelligence test. People interested in joining the Paras can attend a special "insight" weekend. This is run at the Paras headquarters in Aldershot, England. The weekend introduces you to life in the Paras and lets you watch a shooting demonstration and try some parachute training (on the ground).

The first step toward Para training is the Recruit Selection Center. Here you will be tested for fitness, interviewed by army officers, and undergo a medical examination. Your fitness will be tested even further by the Parachute Regiment Aptitude Course. This is a series of physical exercises that help the recruiters see whether you are fit enough to begin the proper Paras training. (The tests are: 15 sit-ups on a bench, 10 dips on the parallel bar, 10 underarm heaves to the bar, a five-mile run, and a one-and-two-thirds–mile/2.5-km steeplechase course over obstacles.) If you get through this successfully, you can then go on to the full Paras recruit training.

For young people around 16 years old who have just left school, there are opportunities to join the Army Foundation College. This is a teaching college that lets students gain further qualifications, but at the same time do military training. After they finish the College, they can go on to serve for three years in the Army if they wish.

For further information on the Parachute Regiment call: +44 (0)1252 349621

USEFUL WEBSITES

The Parachute Regiment's website is at:
http://www.army.mod.uk/infantry/para
Other useful websites are:
http://www.homestead.com/parachuteregiment
http://www.parachute-regiment.com

FURTHER READING

Brehm, Jack. *That Others May Live: The True Story of a PJ, a Member of America's Most Daring Rescue Force.* Victoria, Canada: Crown Publications, 2000.

Bridson, Rory. *The Making of a Para.* London: Sidgwick & Jackson, 1985.

Hastings, Max. *The Battle for the Falklands.* London: Pan, 1997.

Hunter, Robin. *True Stories of the Paras: Red Devils at War.* London: Virgin Publishing, 1999.

McNab, Chris. *Endurance Techniques.* London: Brown Books, 2001.

McNab, Chris. *German Paratroopers.* St. Paul, Minn.: MBI, 2000.

Roberts, Harry. *Capture at Arnhem: A Diary of Disaster and Survival.* Gloucester, England: The Windrush Press, 1999.

Stillwell, Alexander. *The Encyclopedia of Survival Techniques.* New York: Lyons Press, 2000.

Weale, Adrian. *Fighting Fit—The Complete SAS Fitness Training Guide.* London: Orion, 2001.

Wiseman, John. *The SAS Personal Trainer.* London: Lewis International Inc., 1998.

ABOUT THE AUTHOR

Dr. Chris McNab has written and edited numerous books on military history and elite forces survival. His publications to date include *German Paratroopers of World War II, The Illustrated History of the Vietnam War, First Aid Survival Manual,* and *Special Forces Endurance Techniques,* as well as many articles and features in other works. Forthcoming publications include books on the SAS, while Chris's wider research interests lie in literature and ancient history. Chris lives in South Wales, U.K.

INDEX

References in italics refer to illustrations